THIS BOOK BELONG TO ....

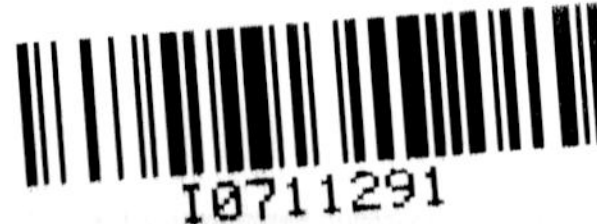

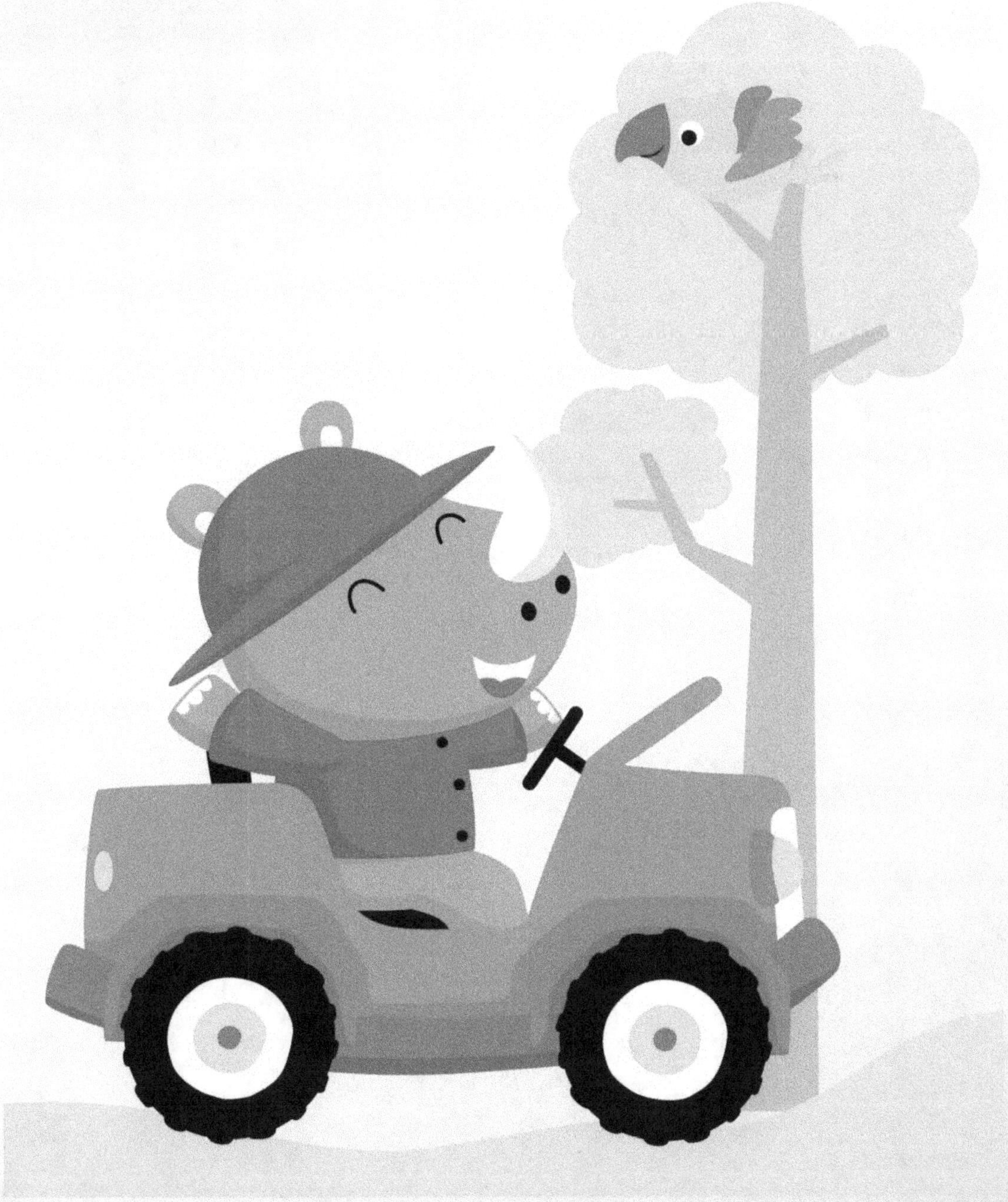

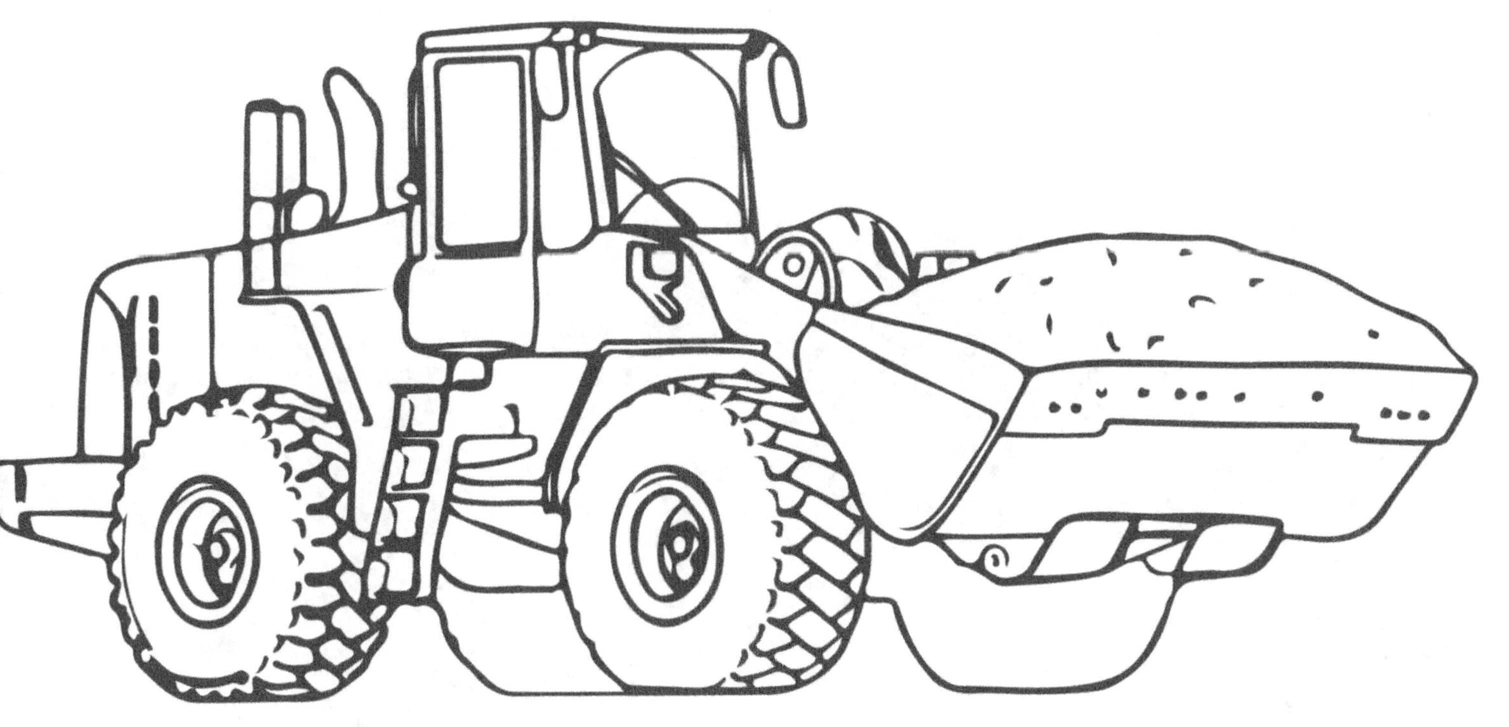

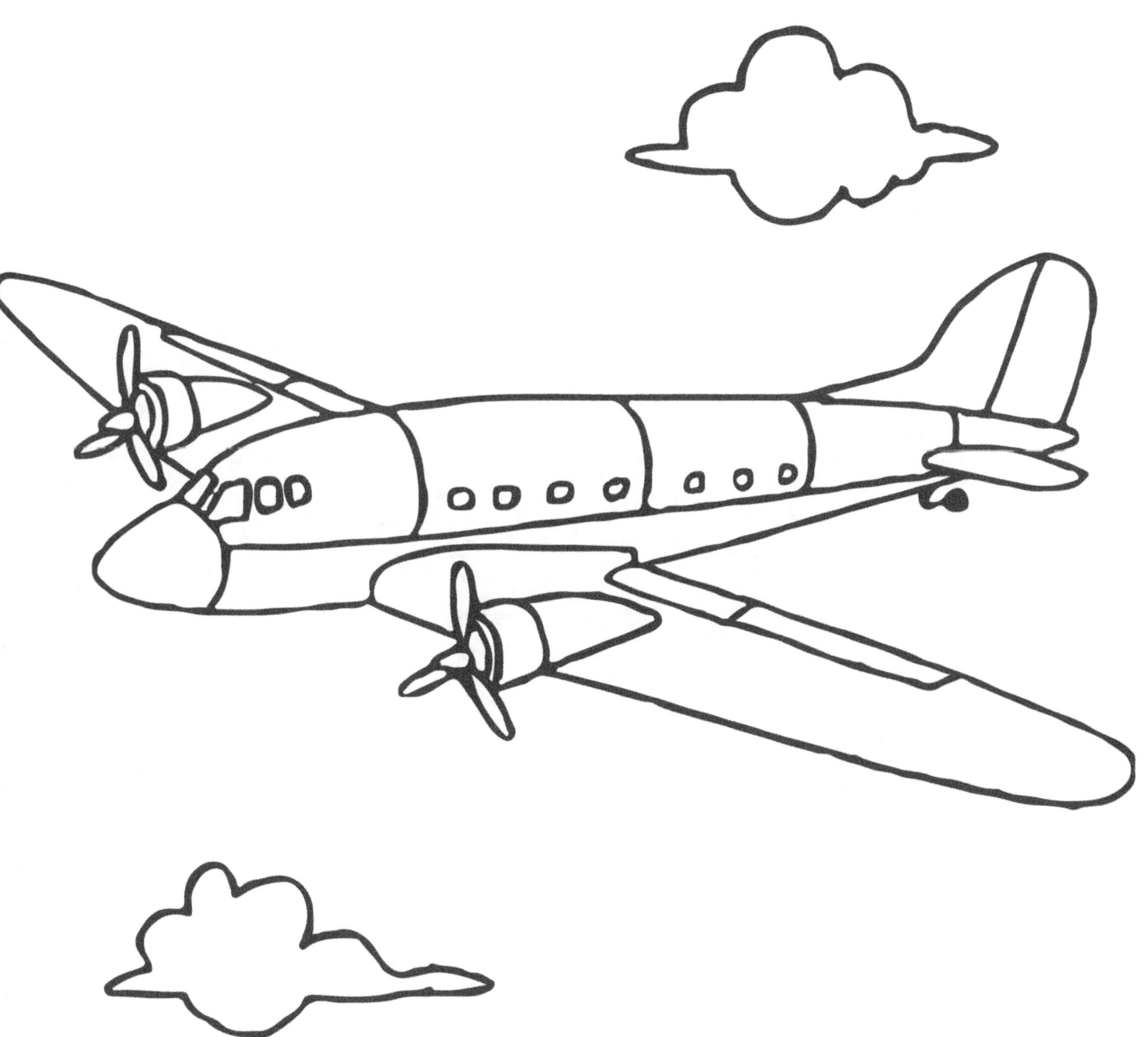

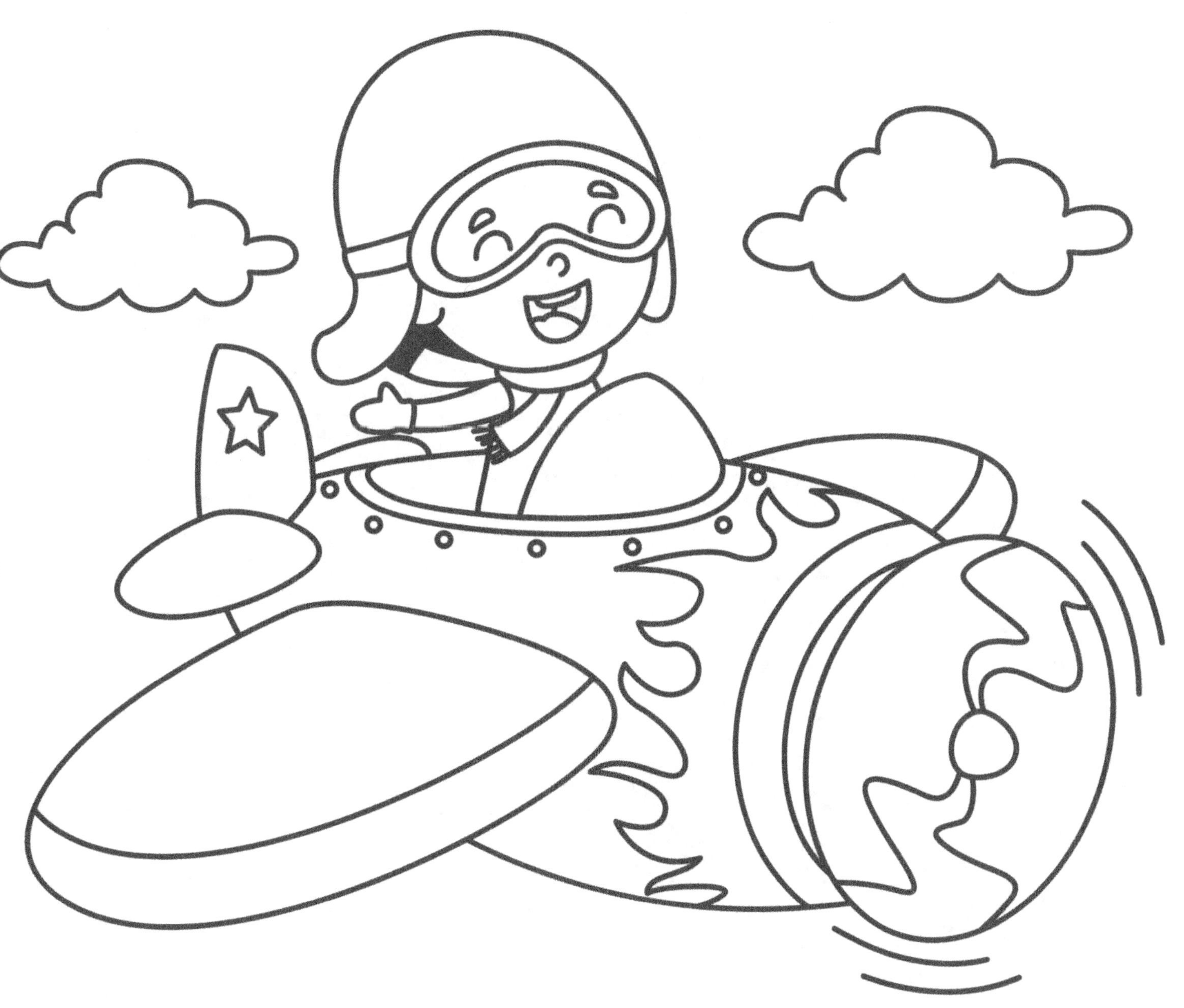

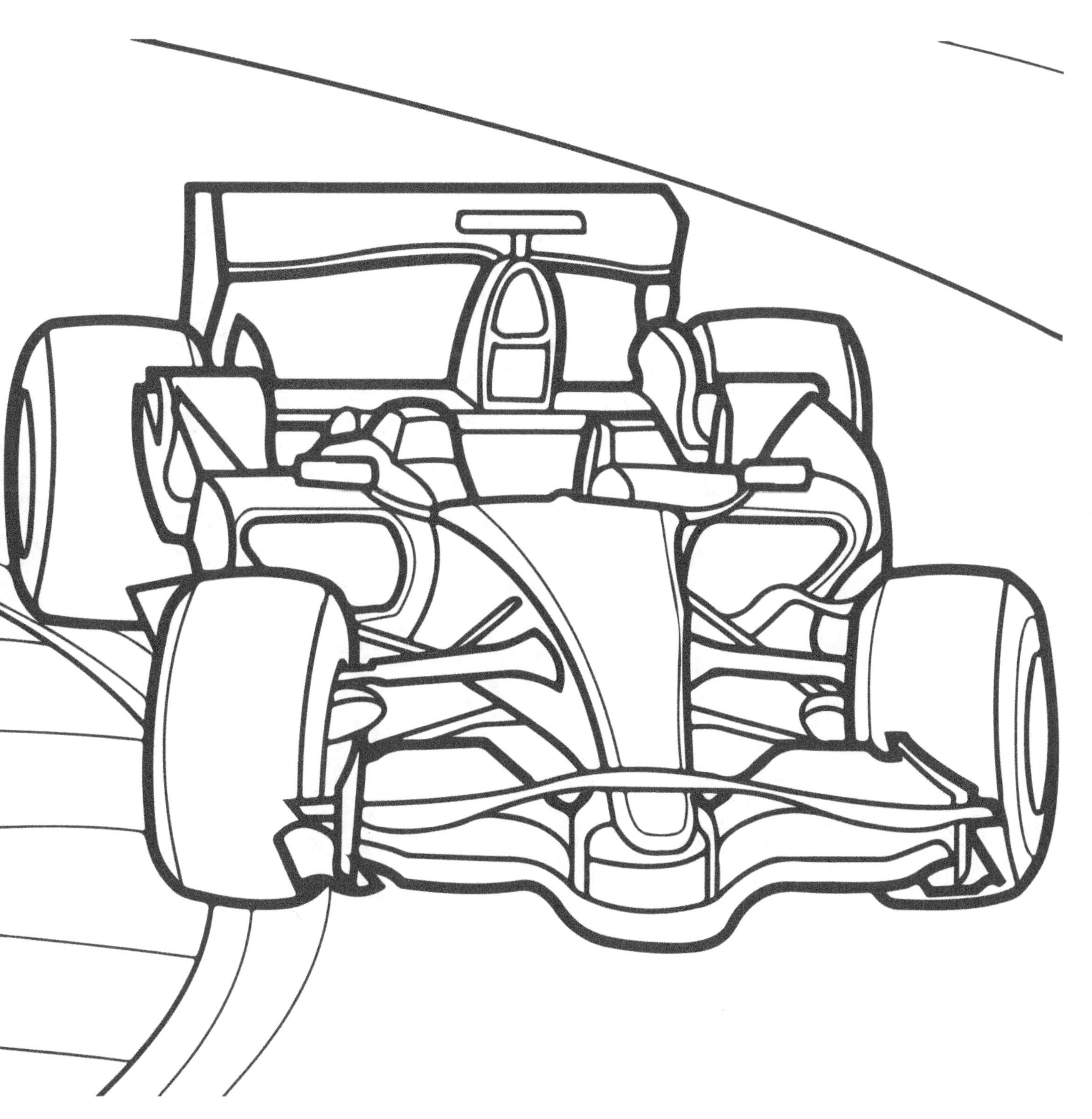

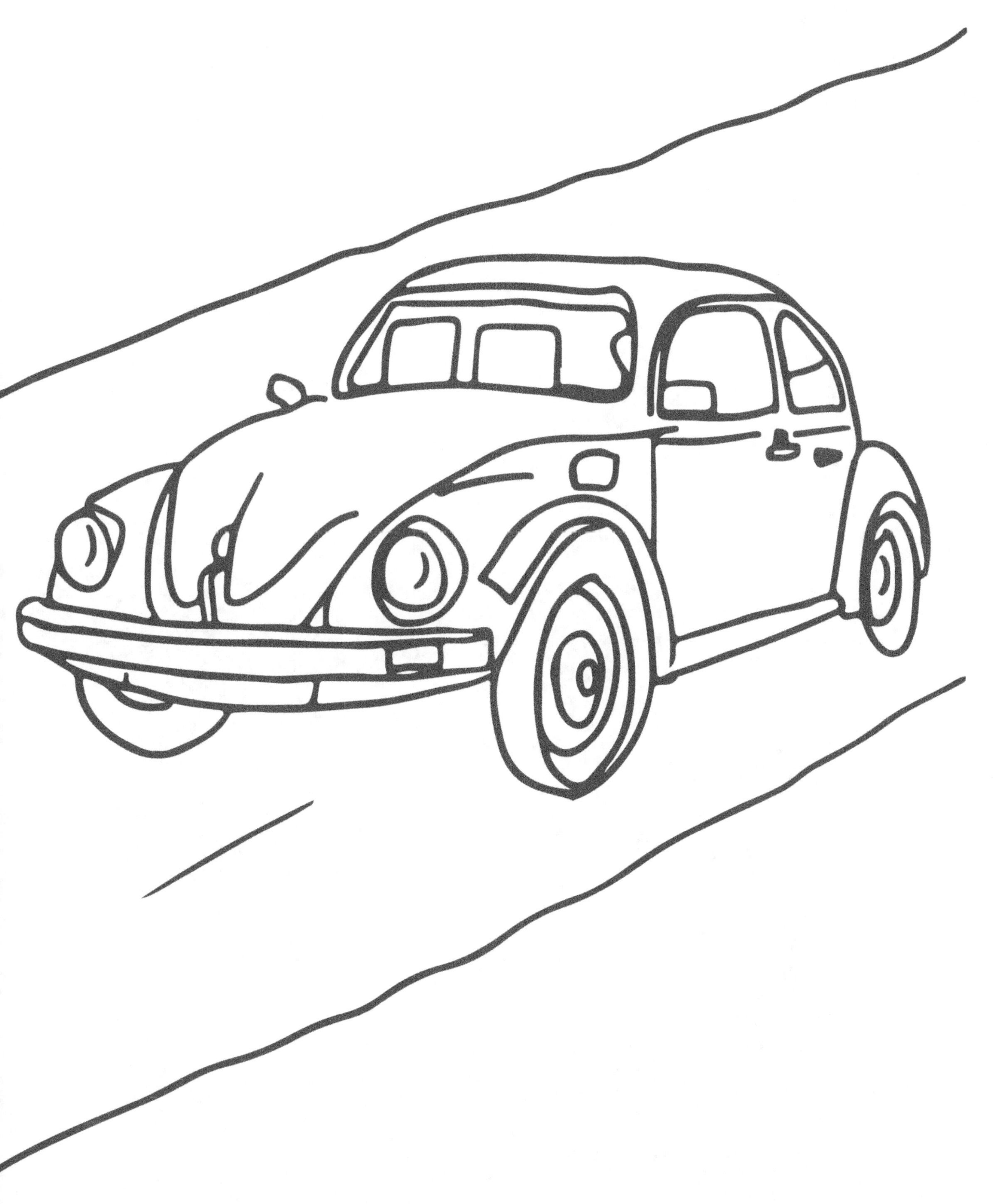

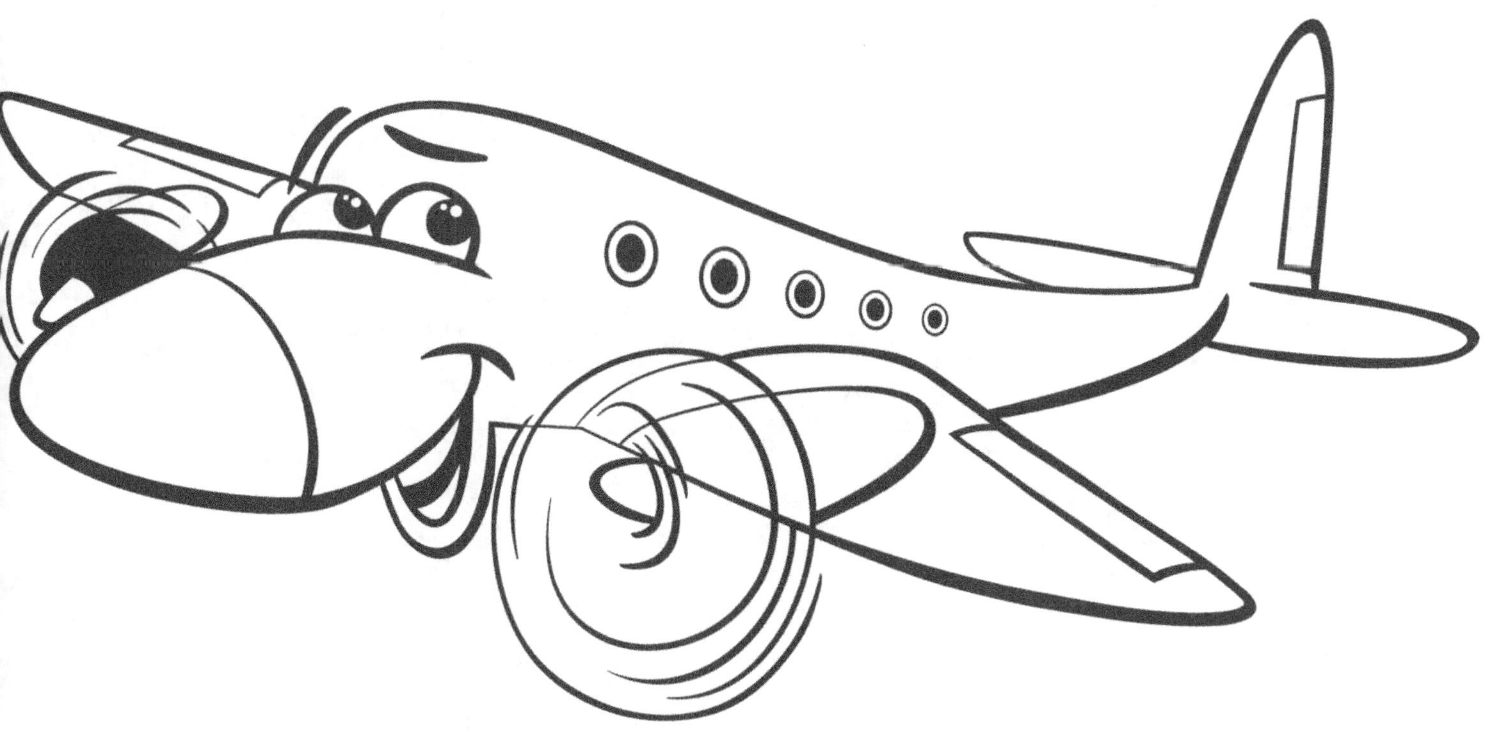

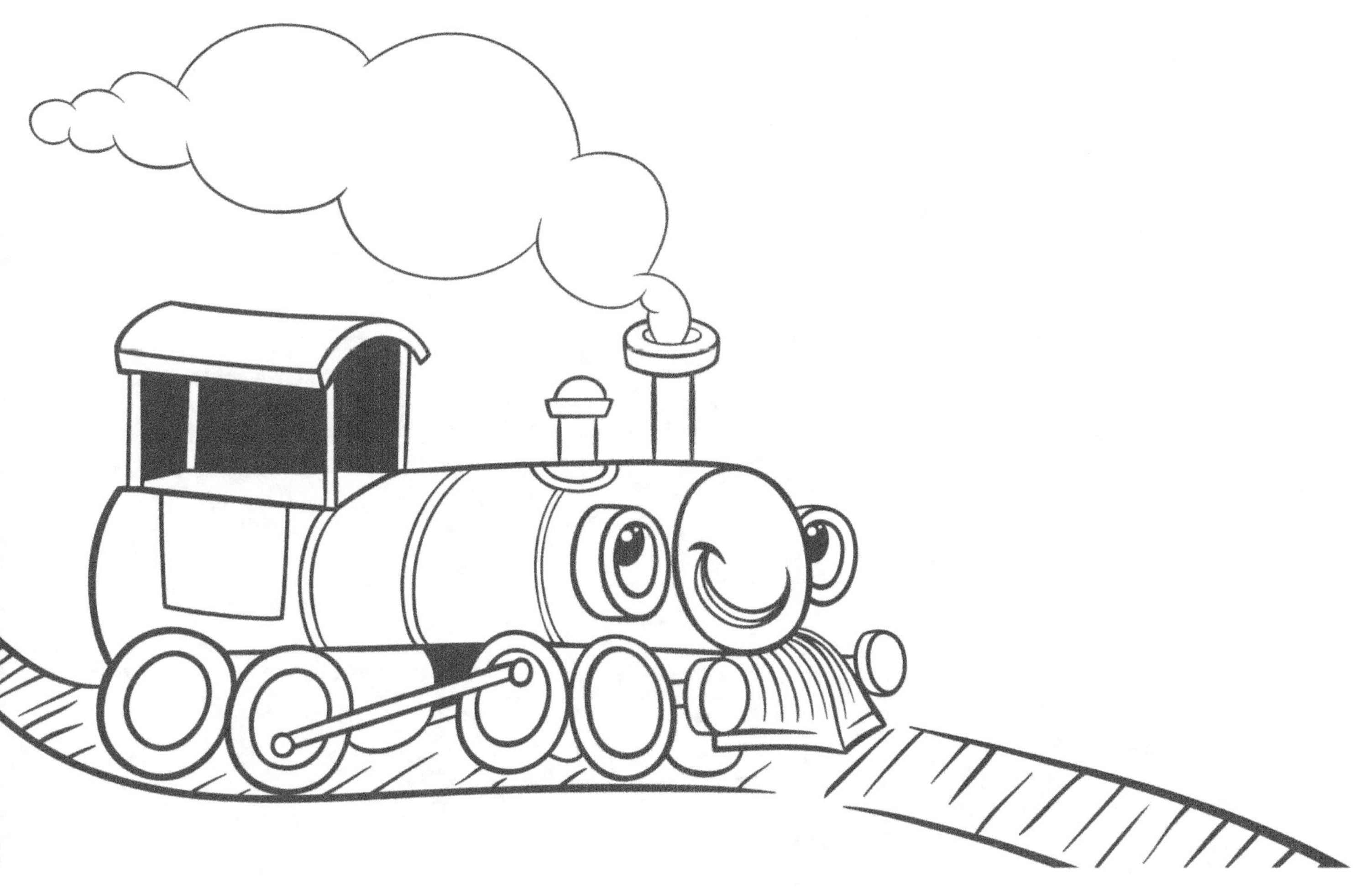

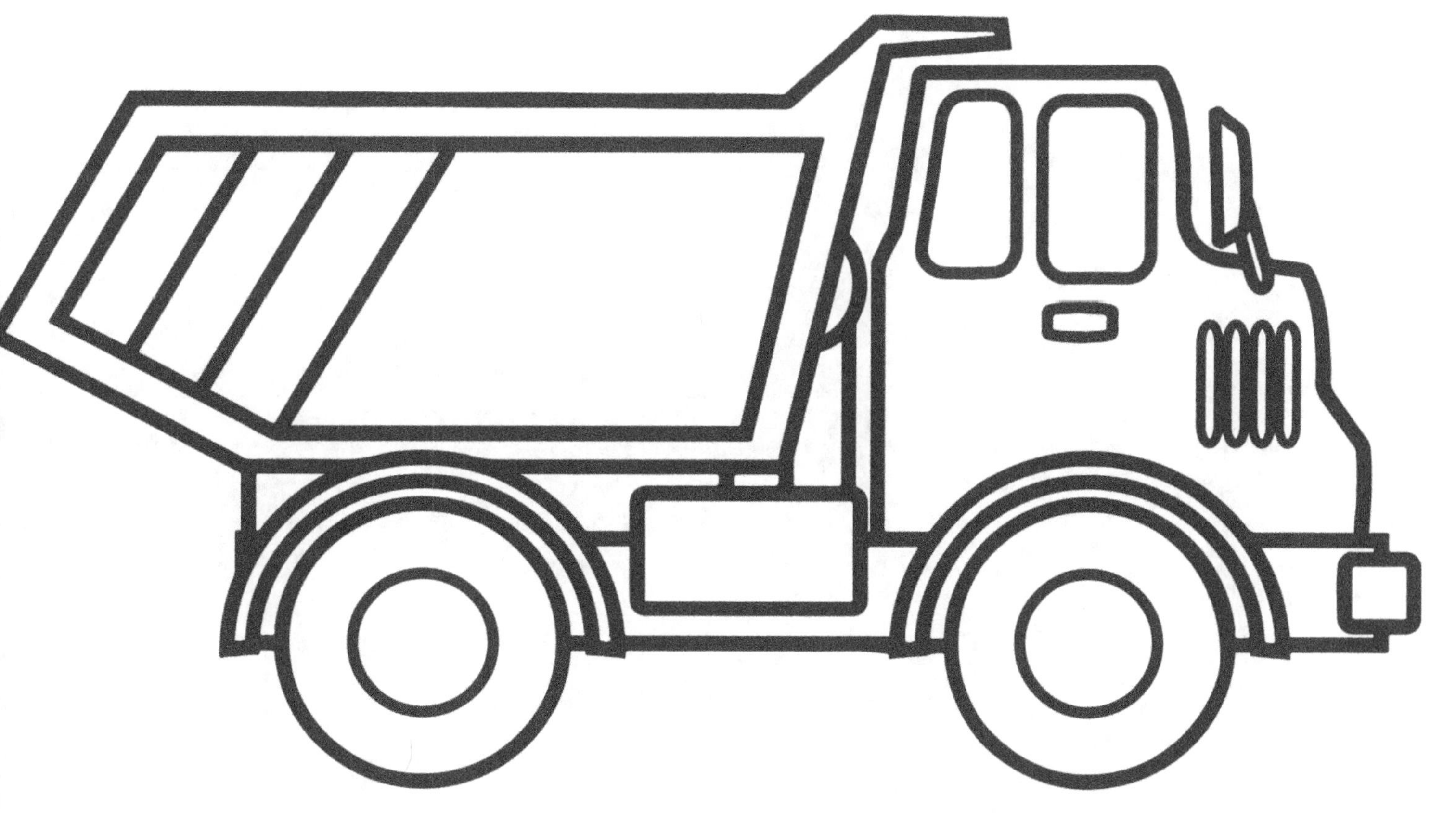

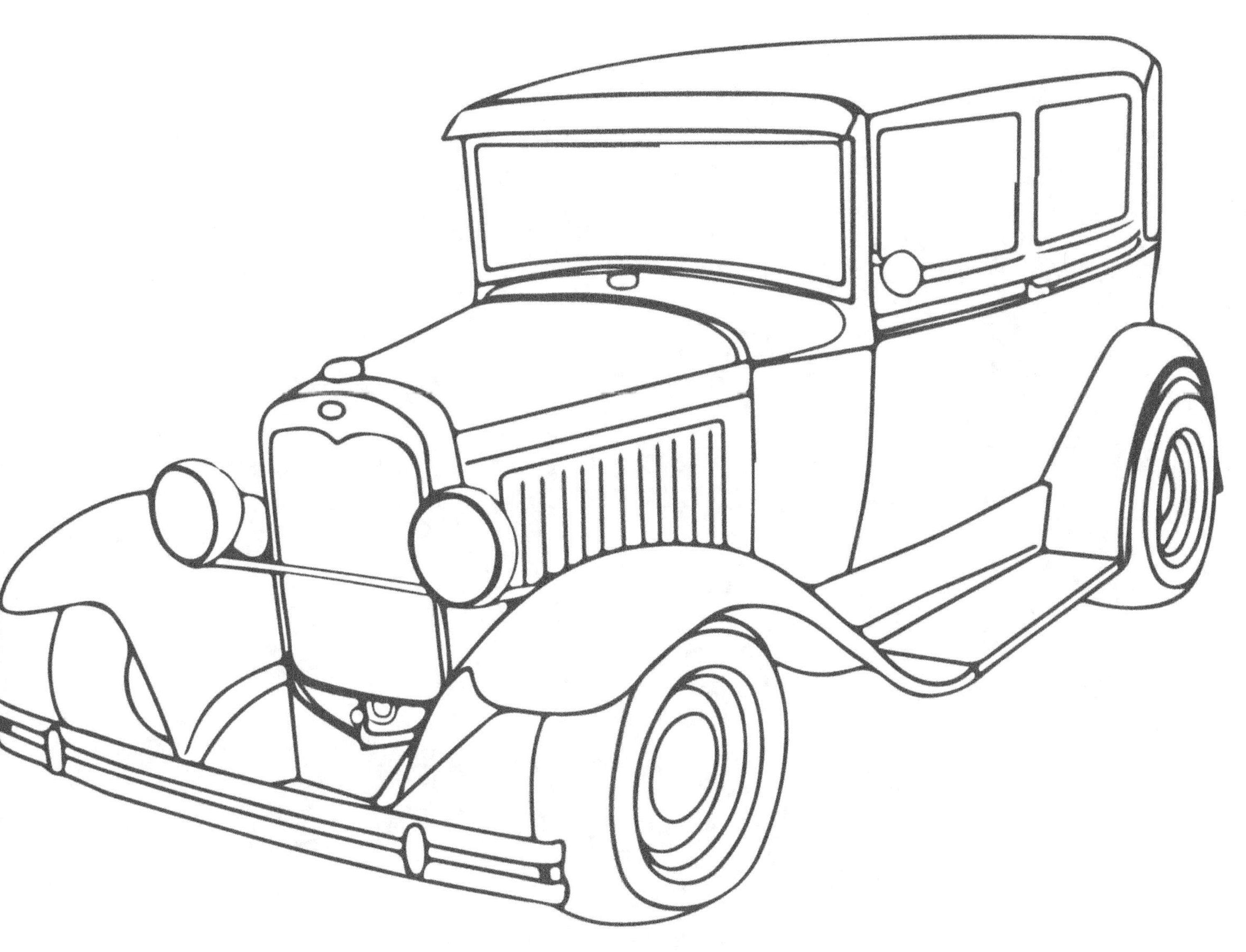

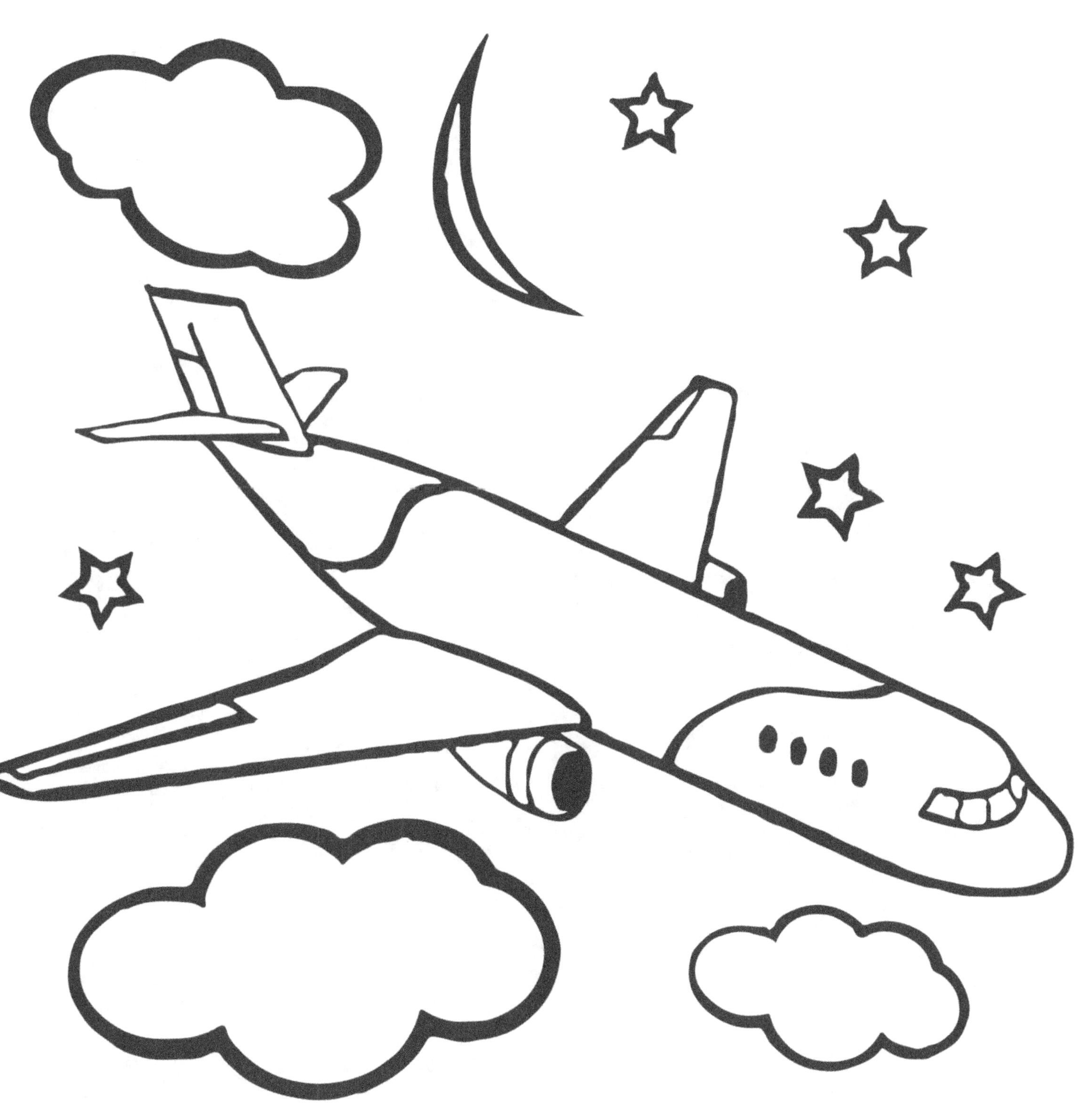

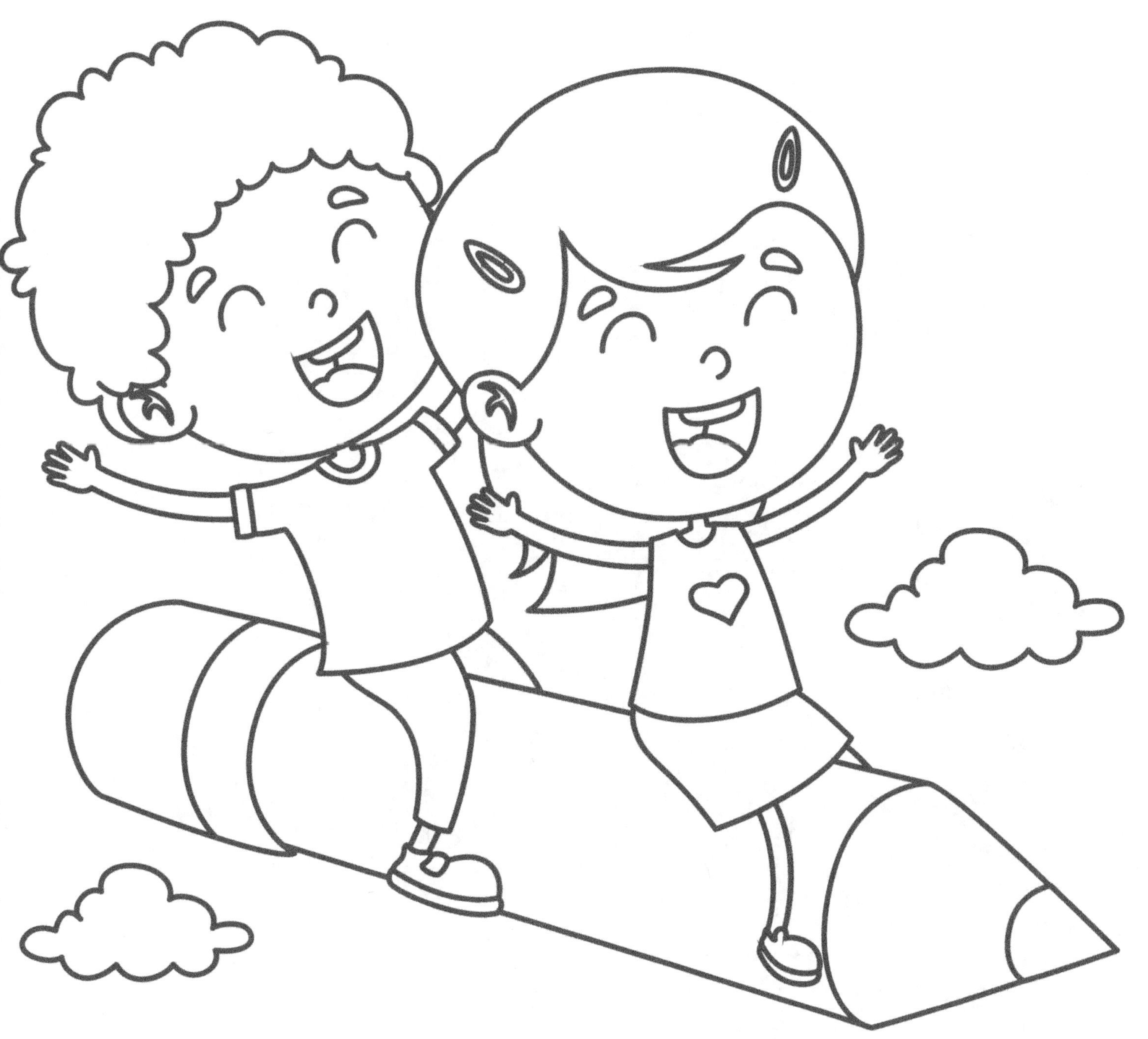

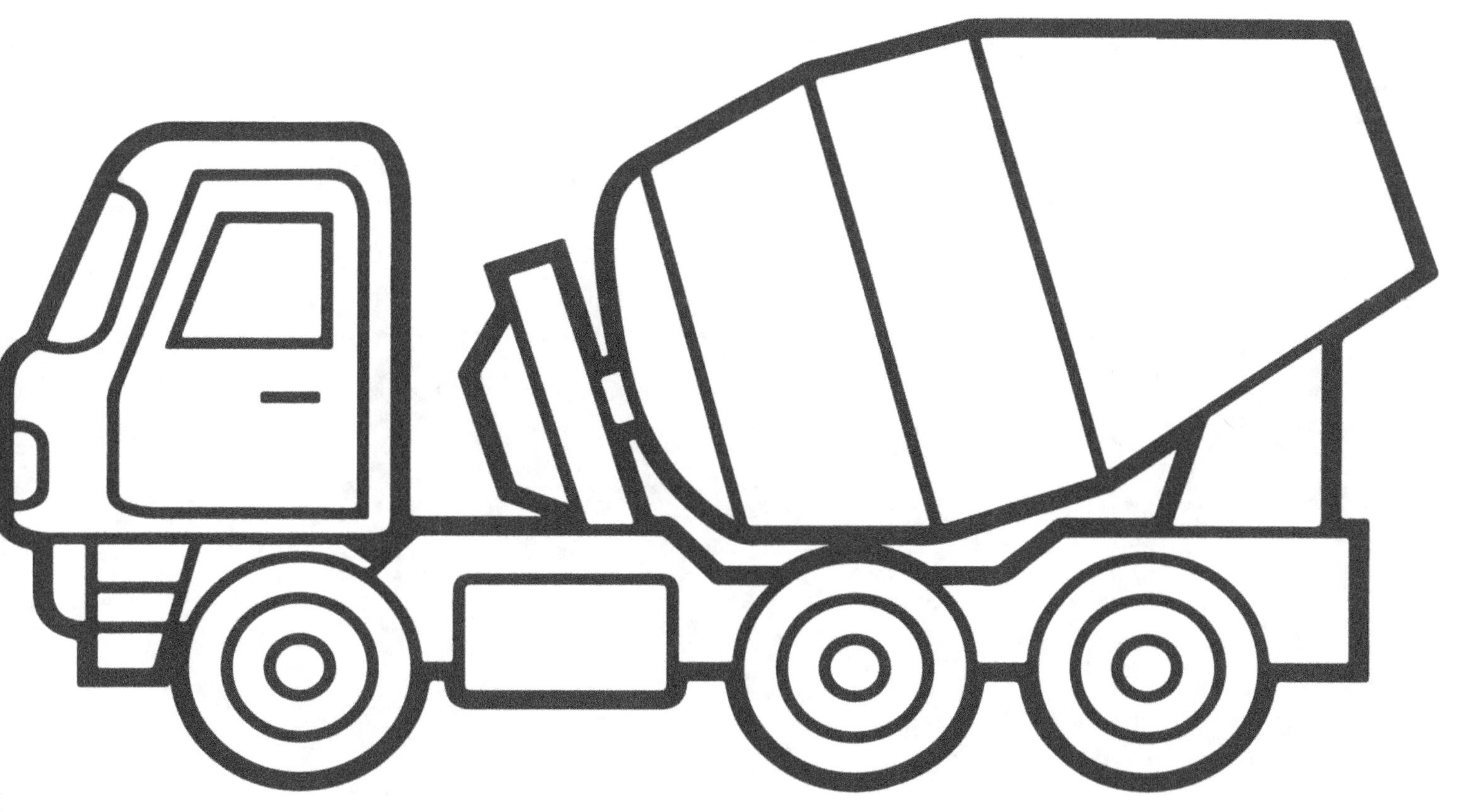

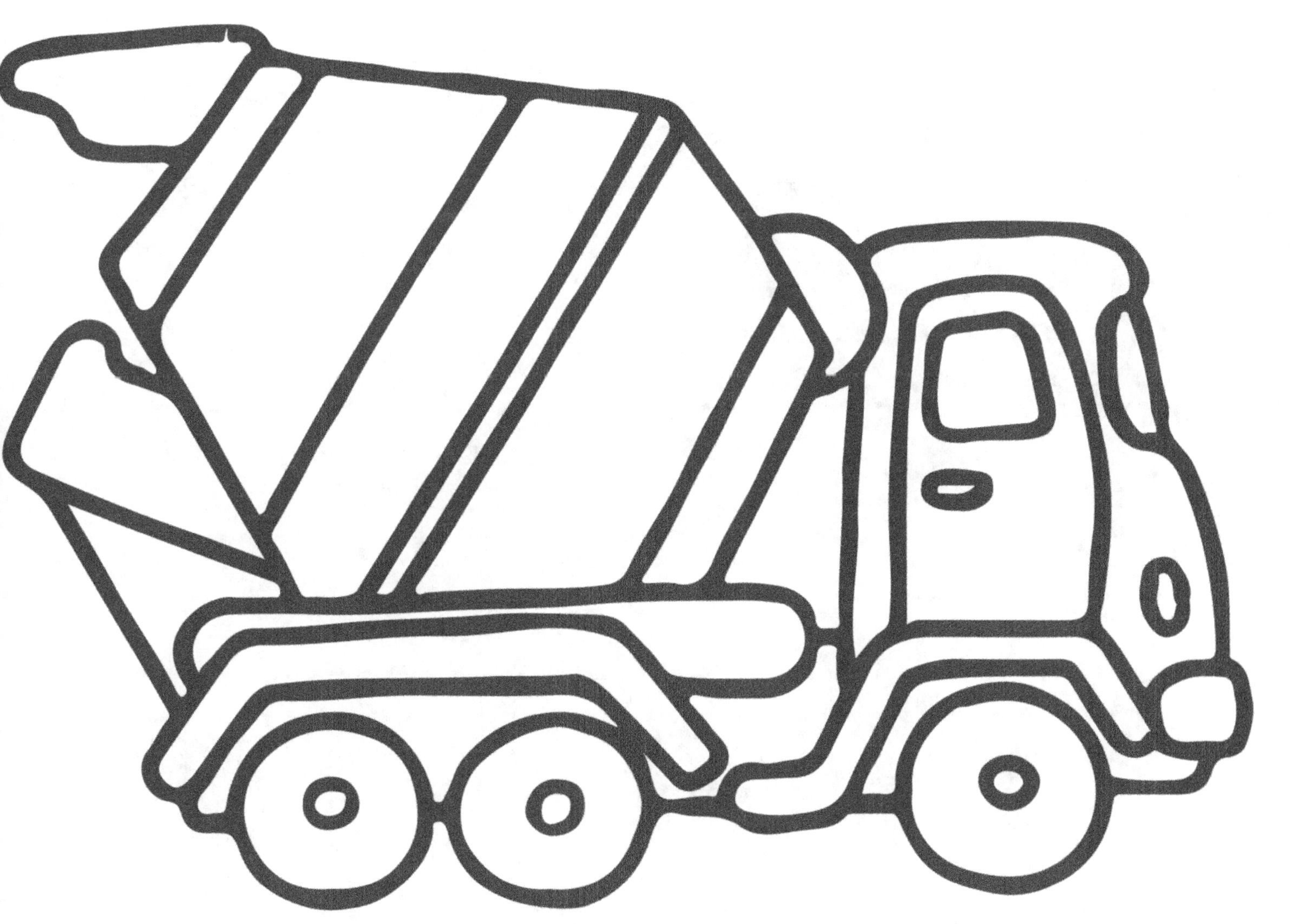

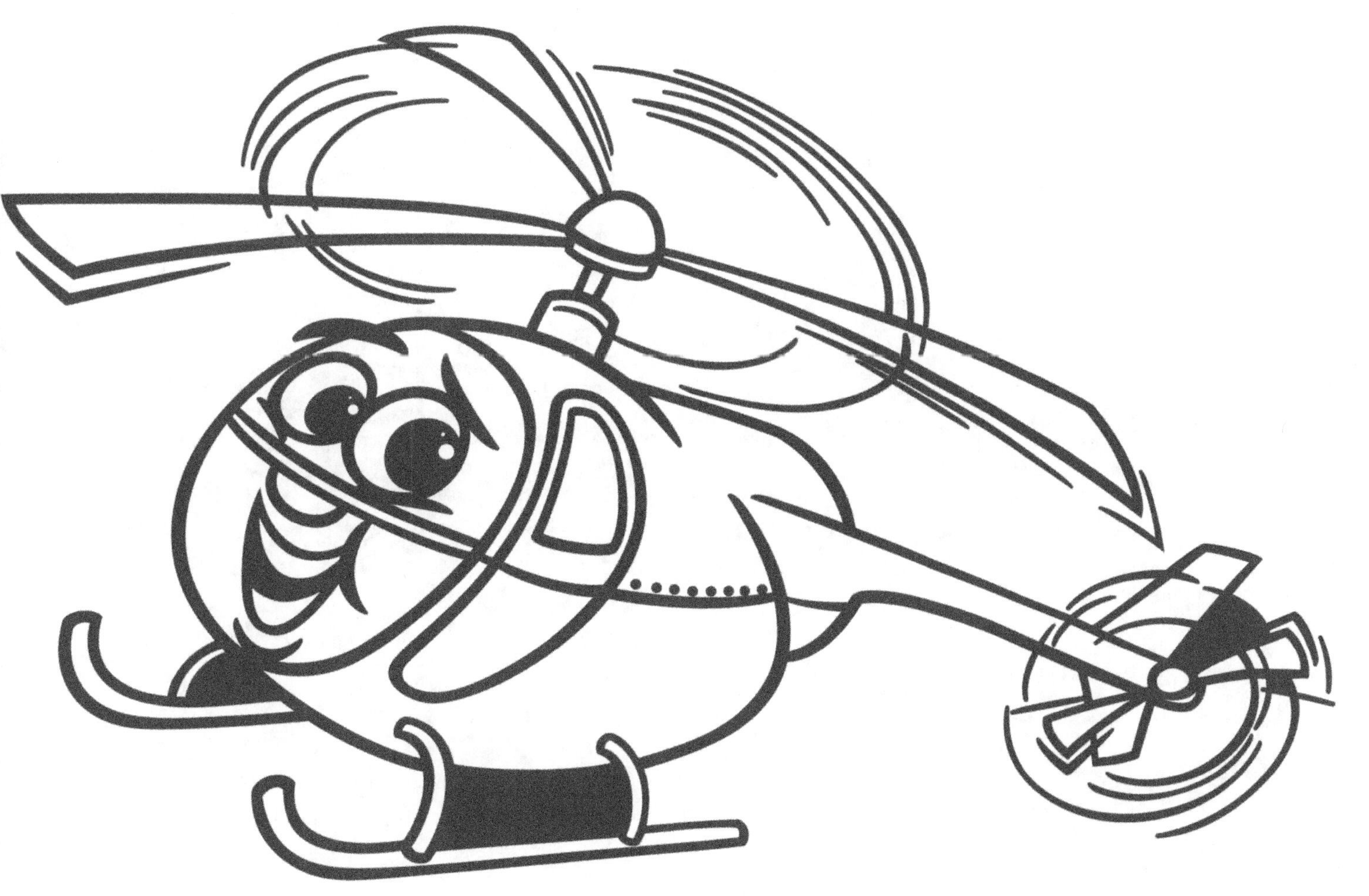

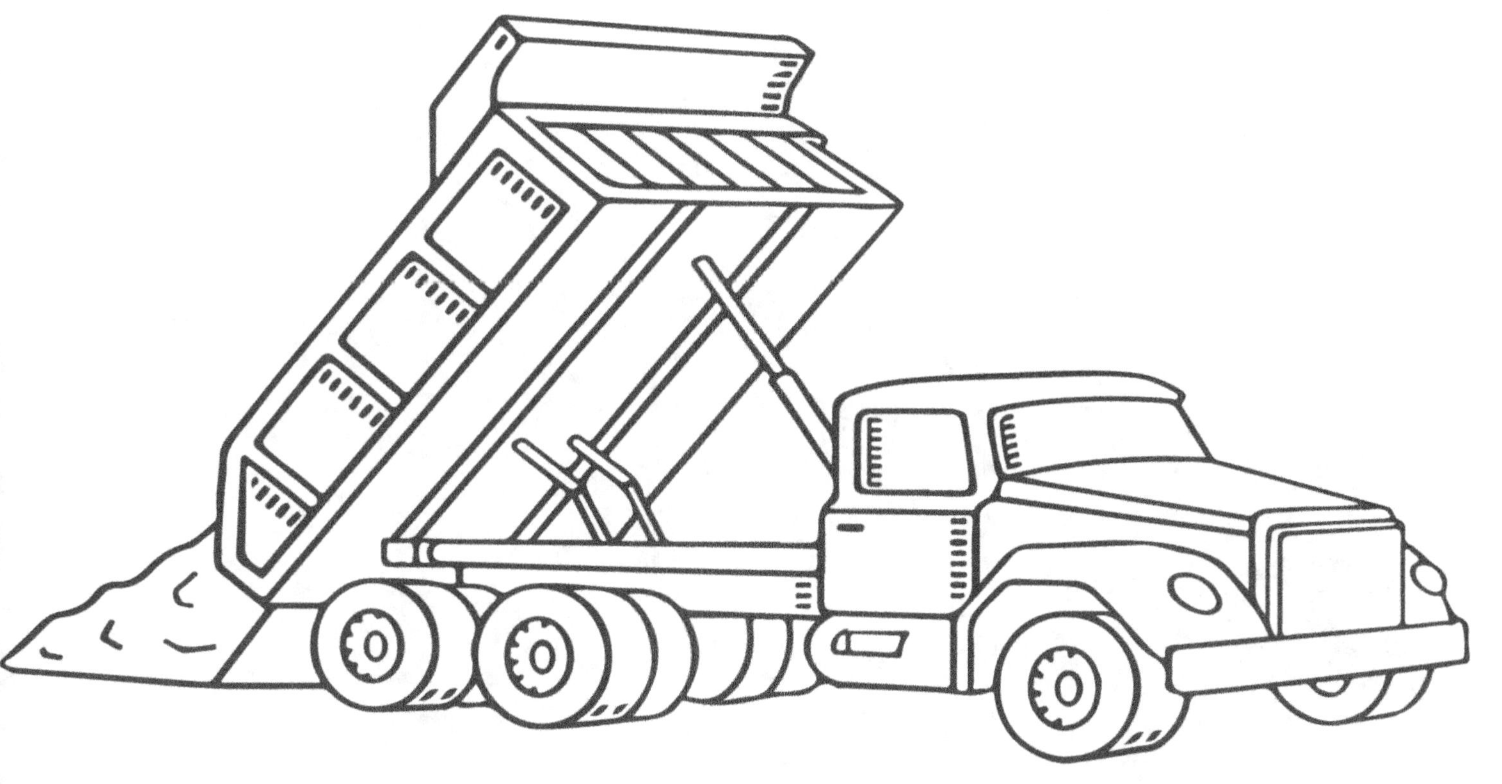

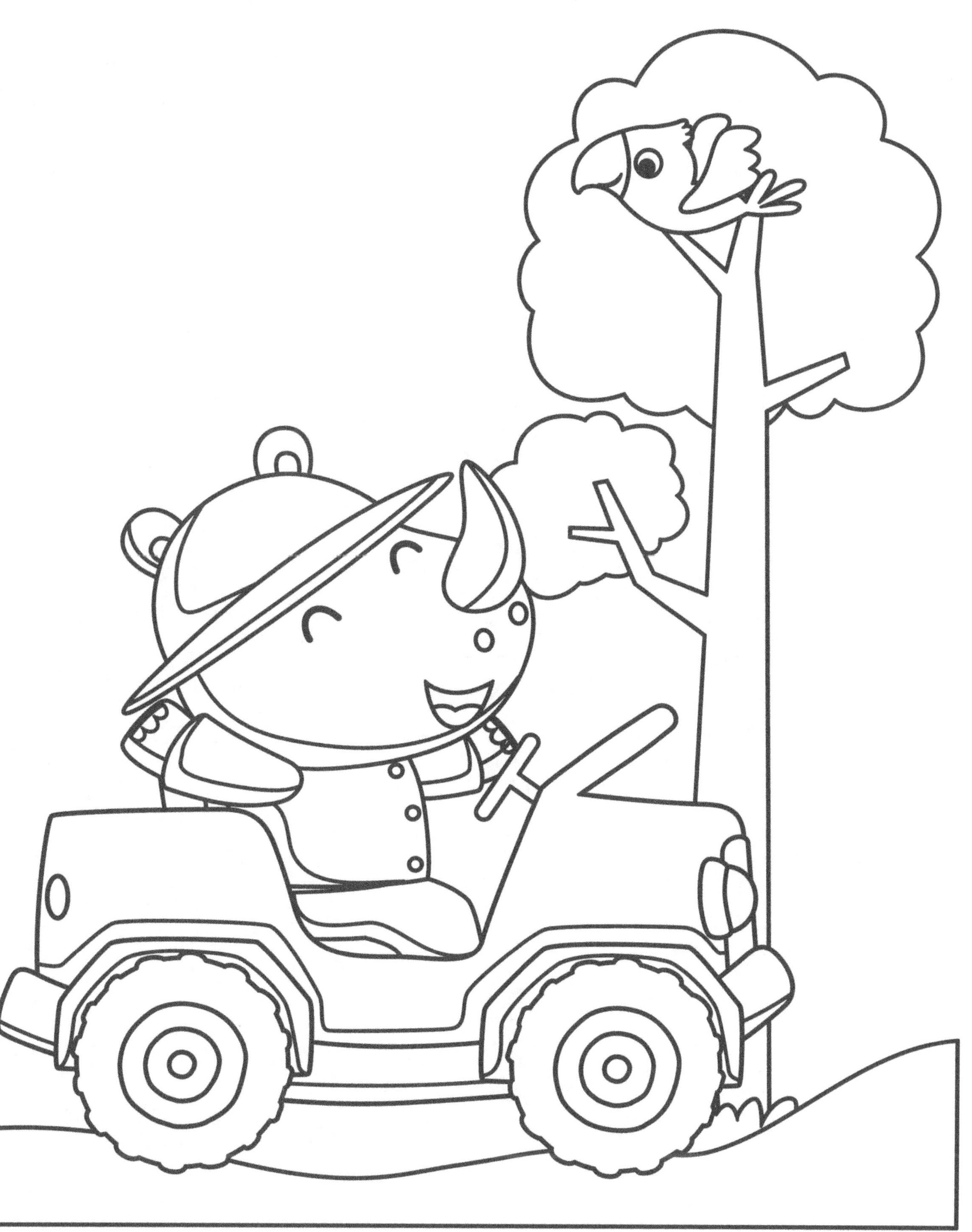

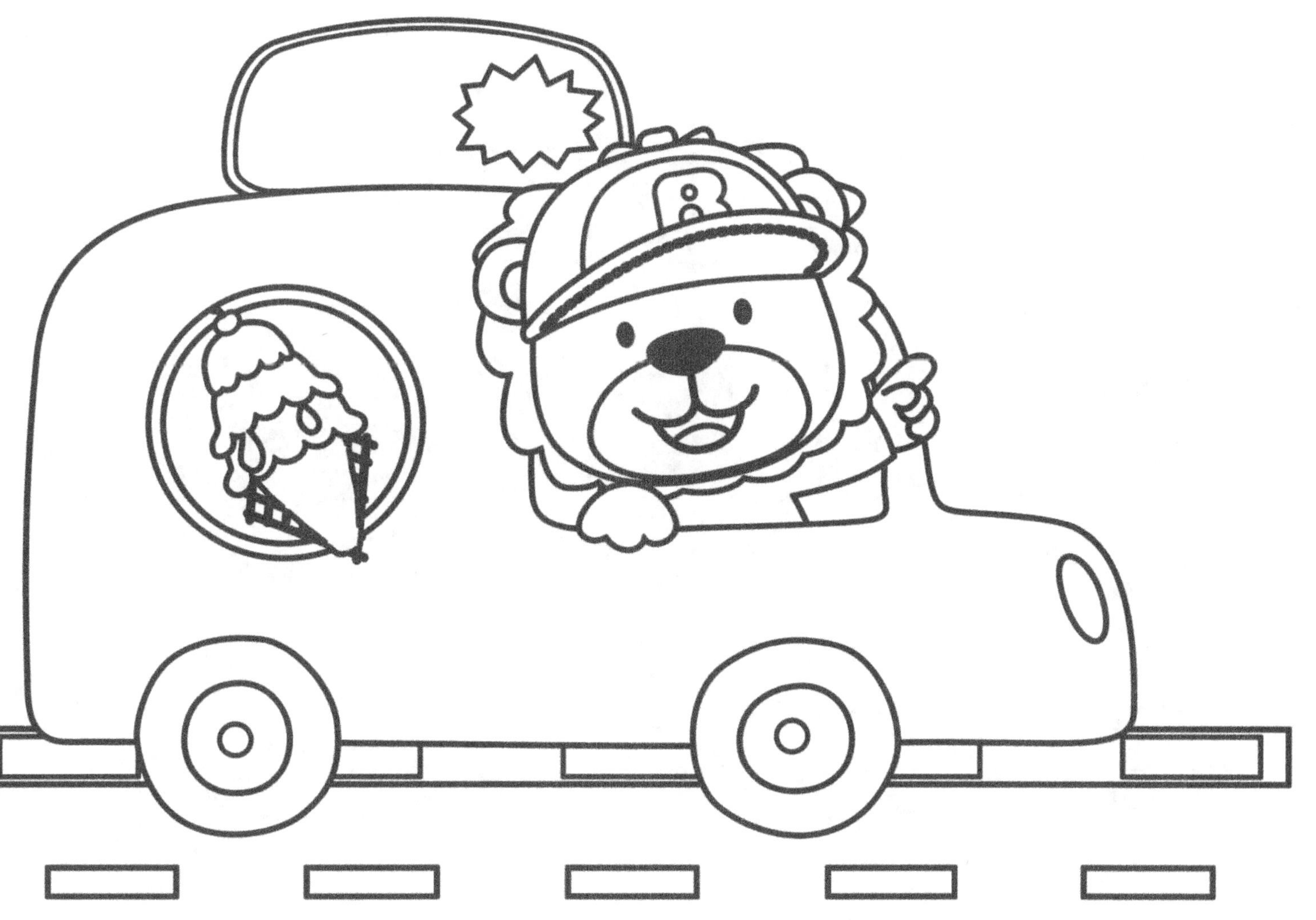

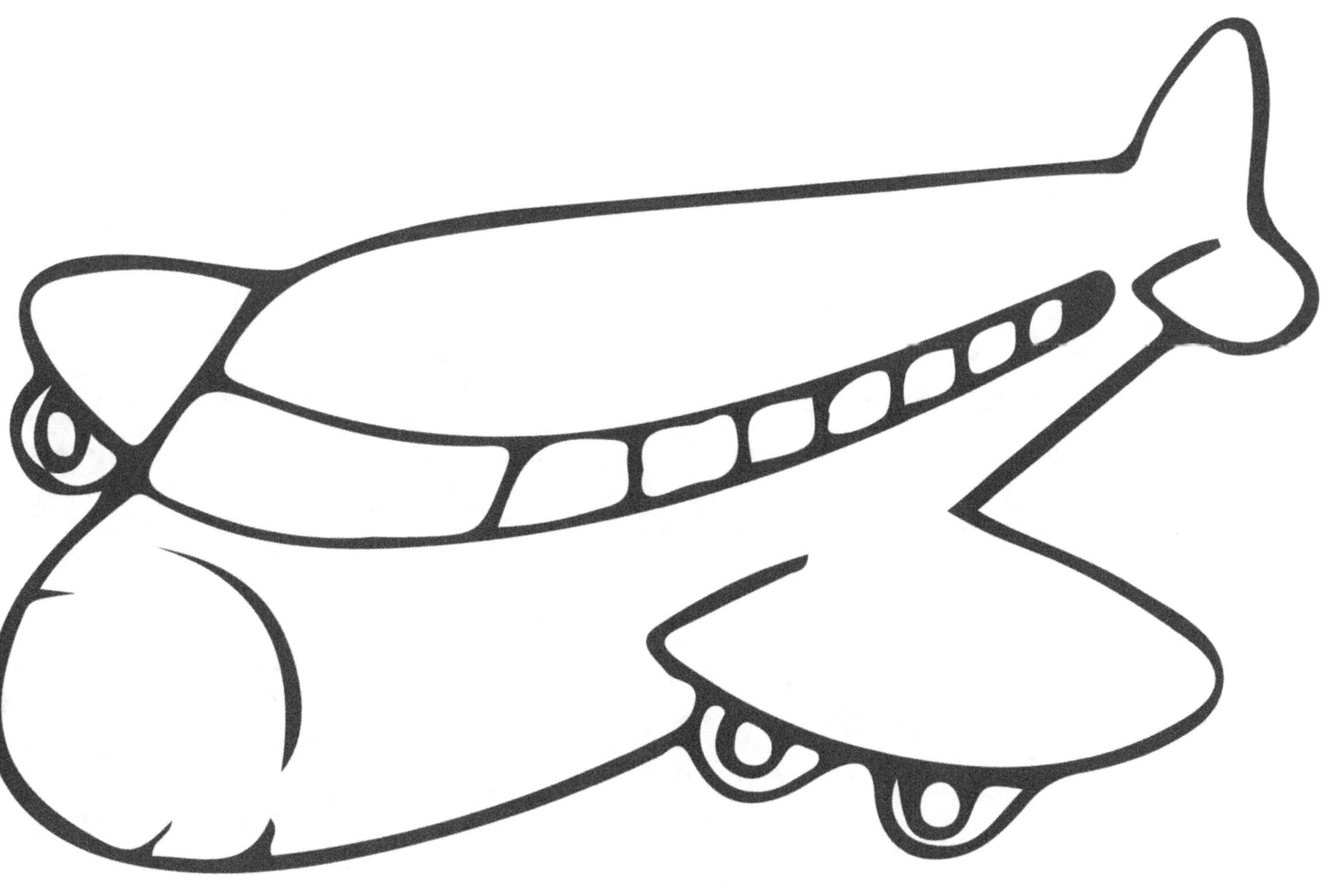

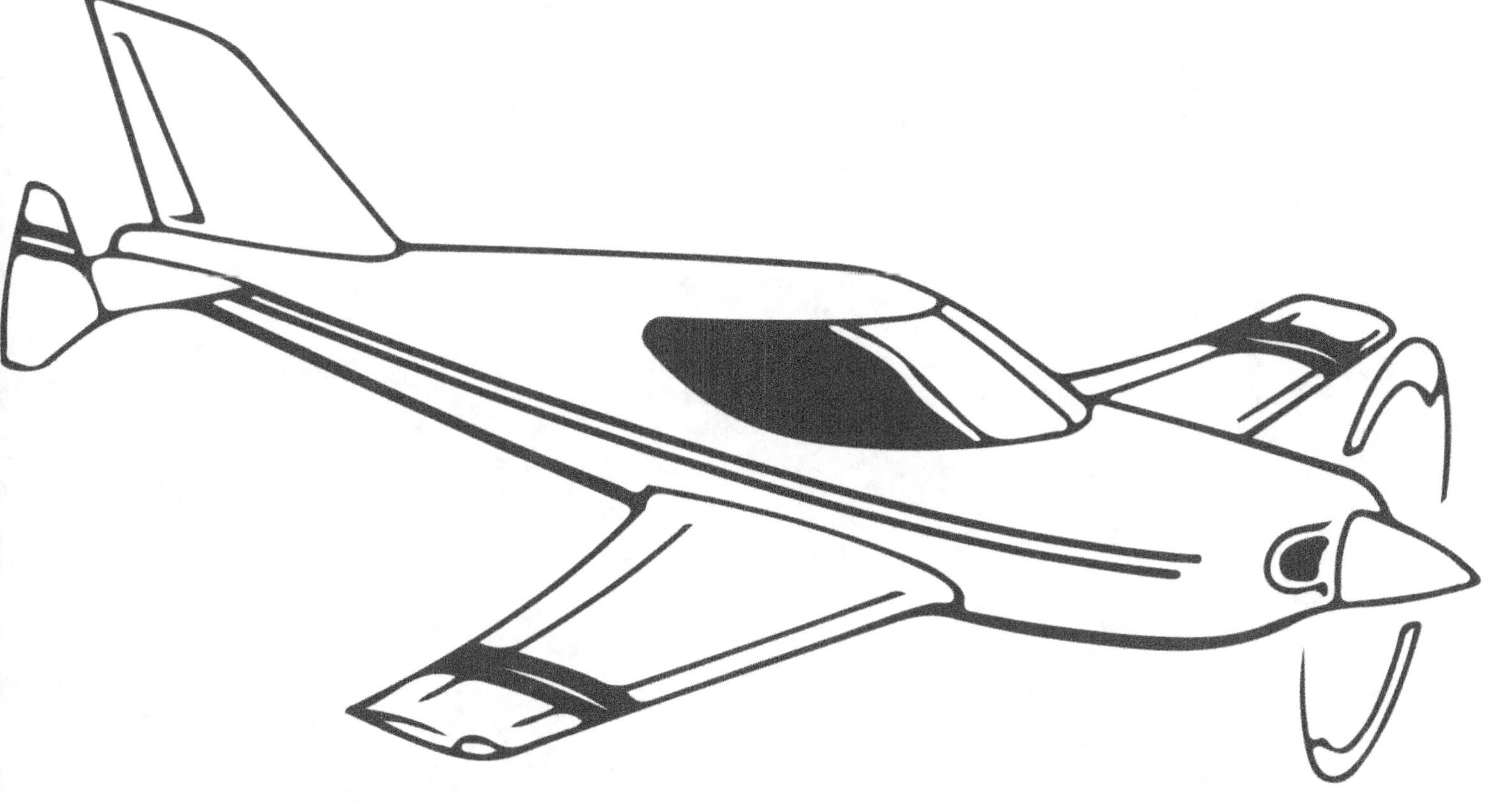

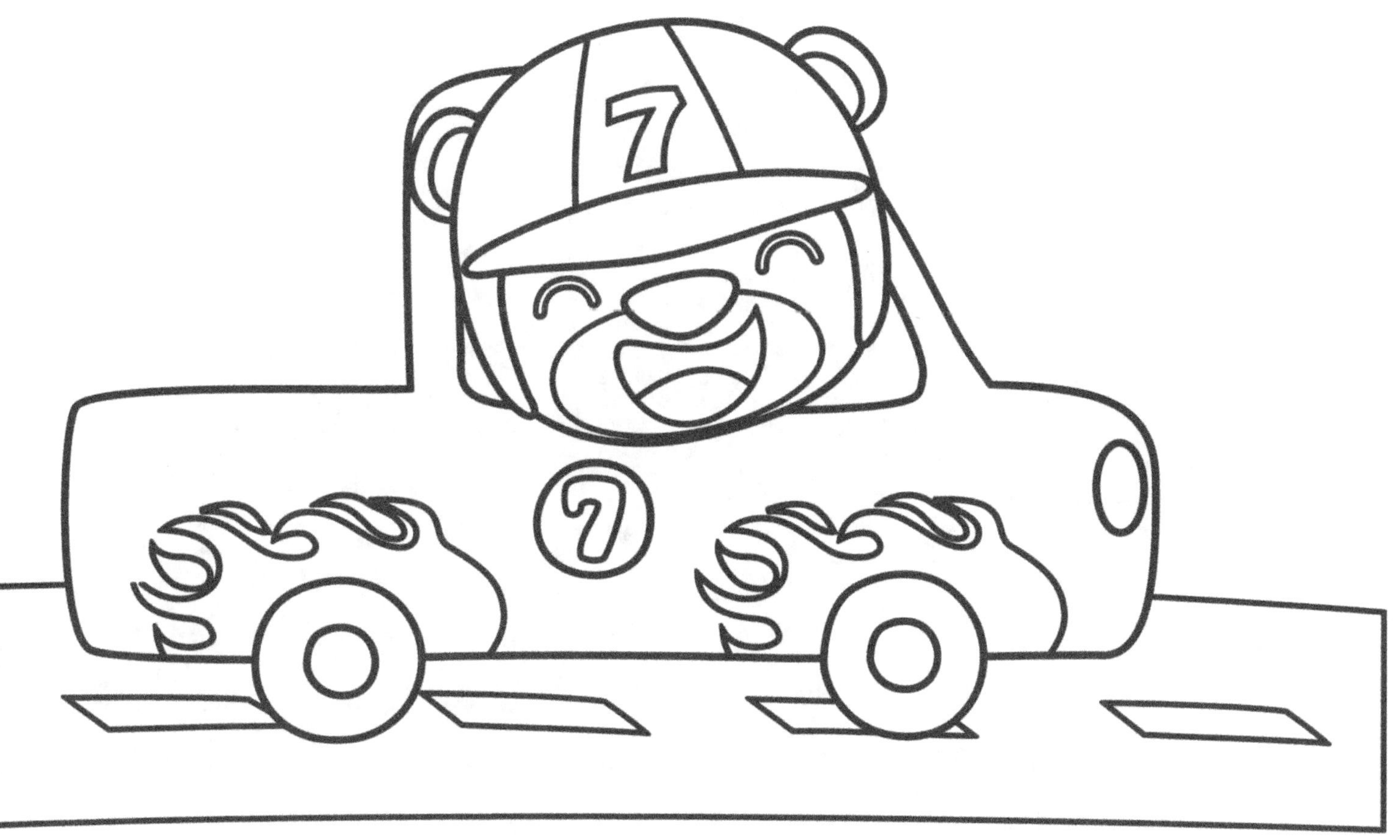

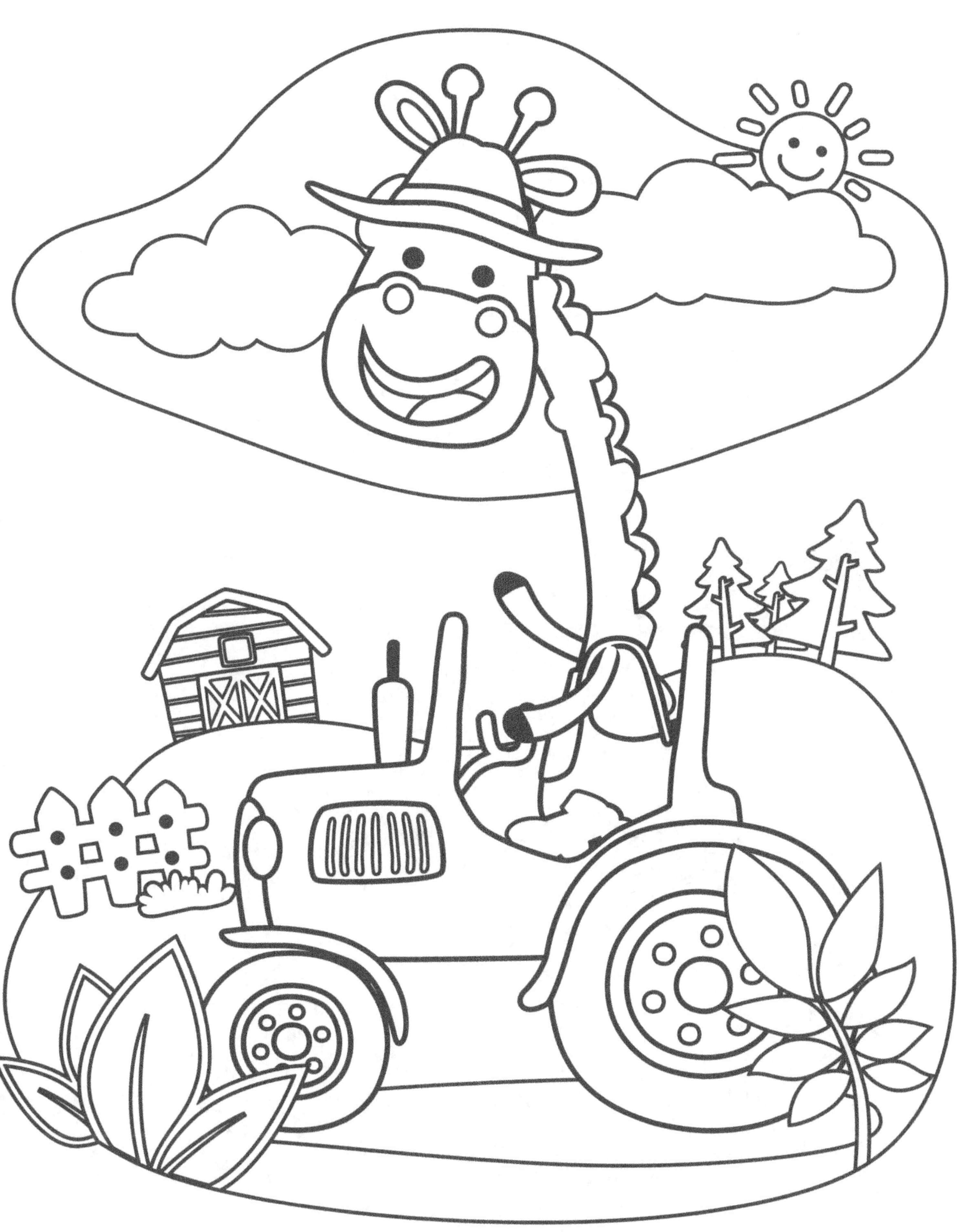

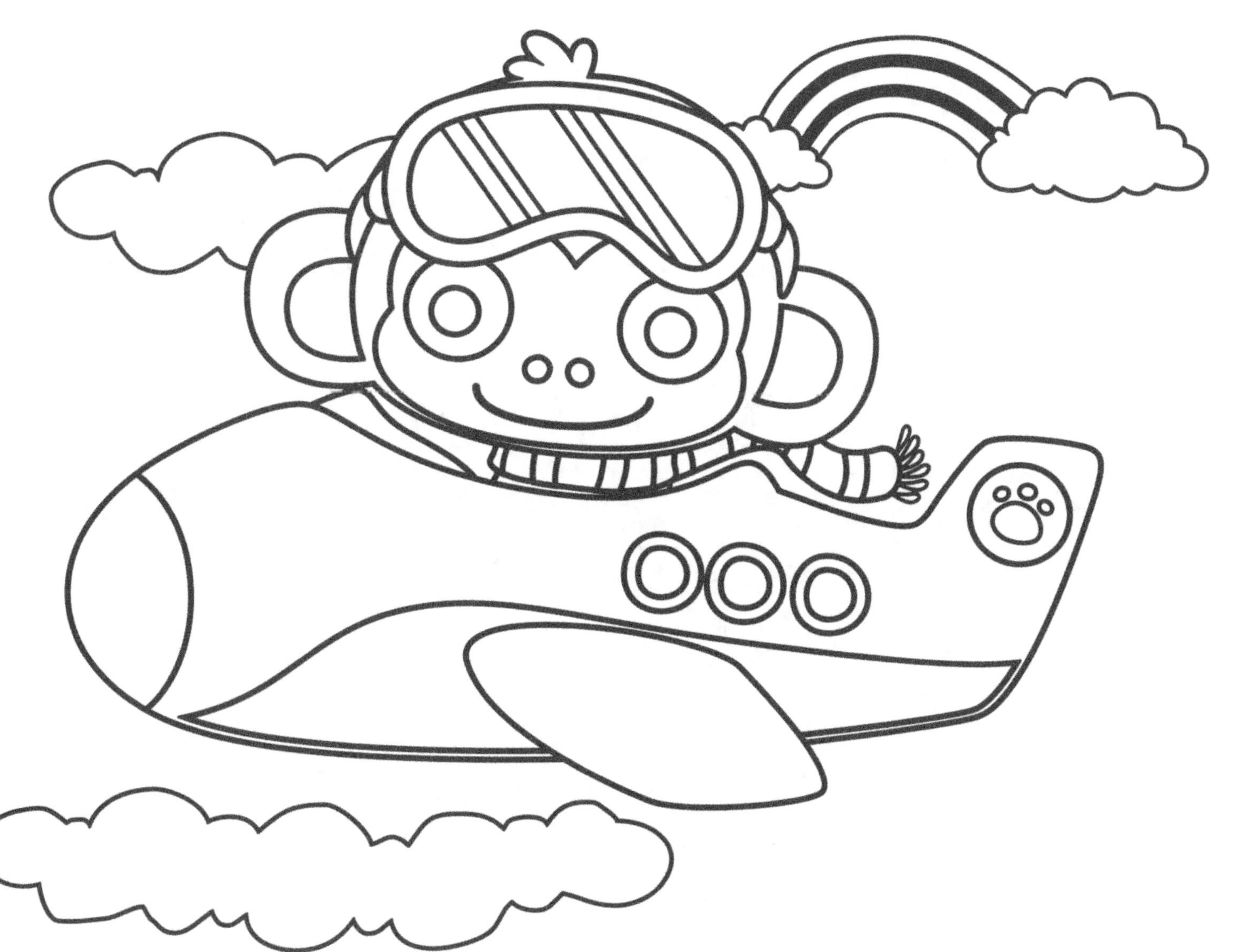

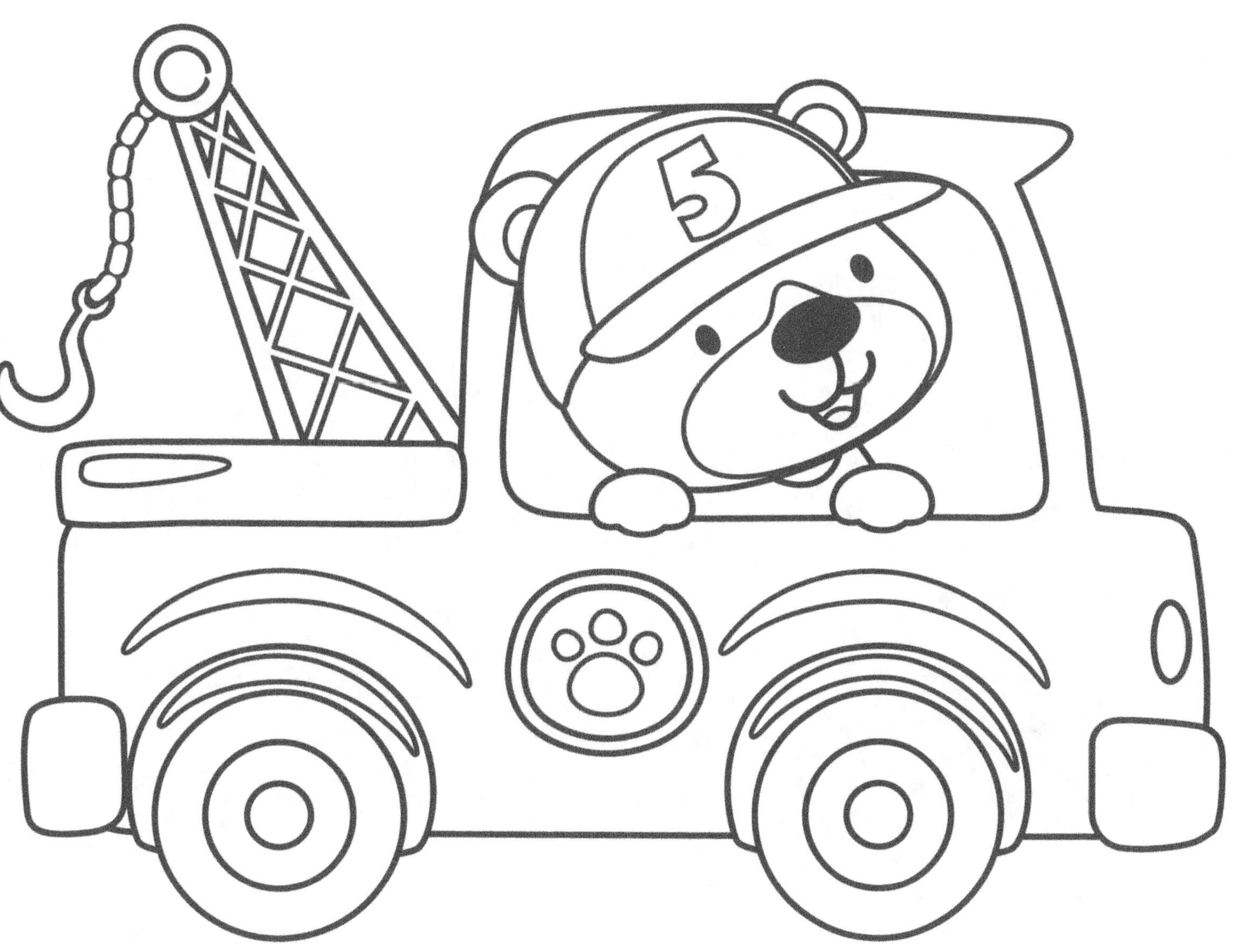
5

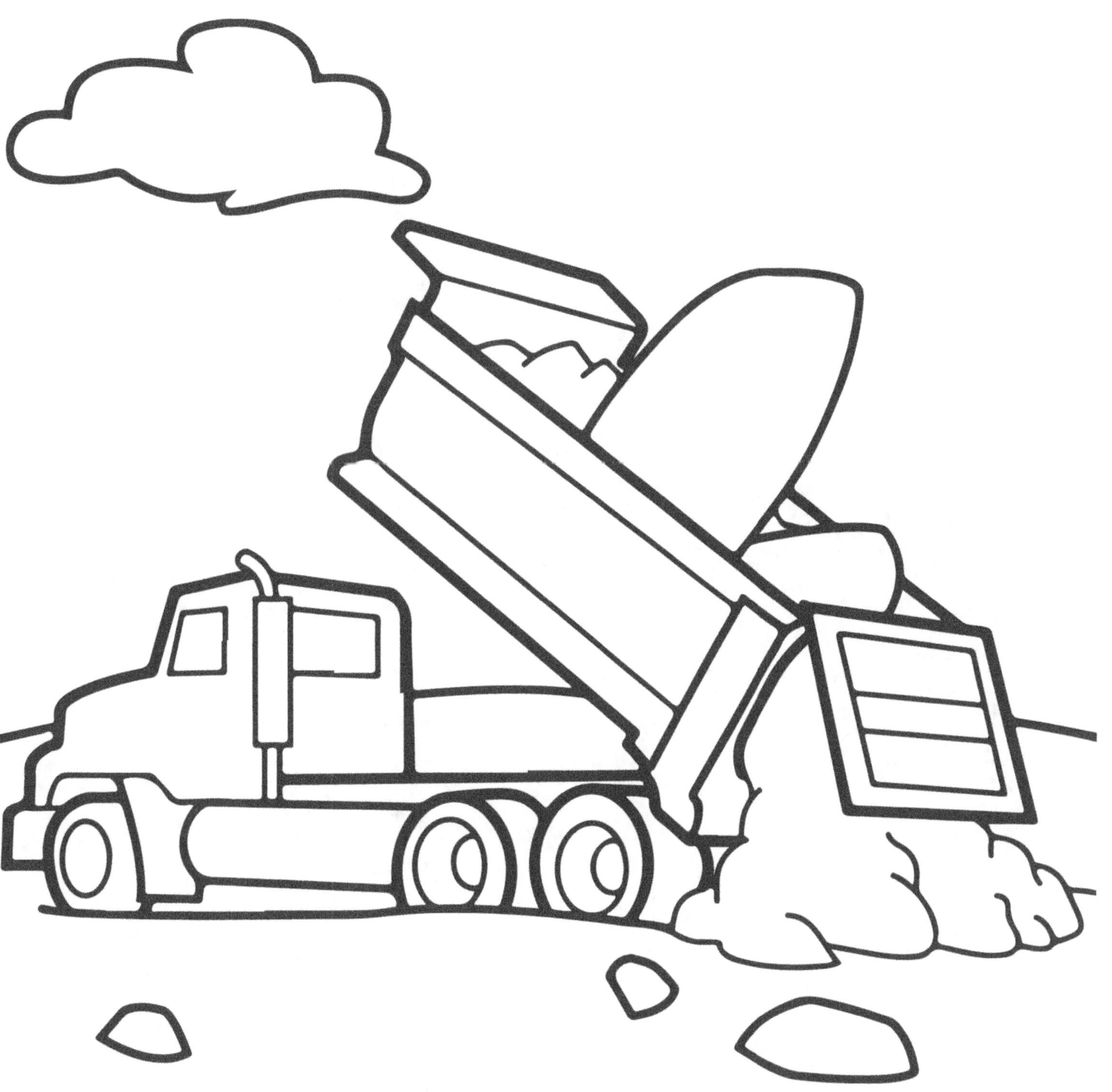

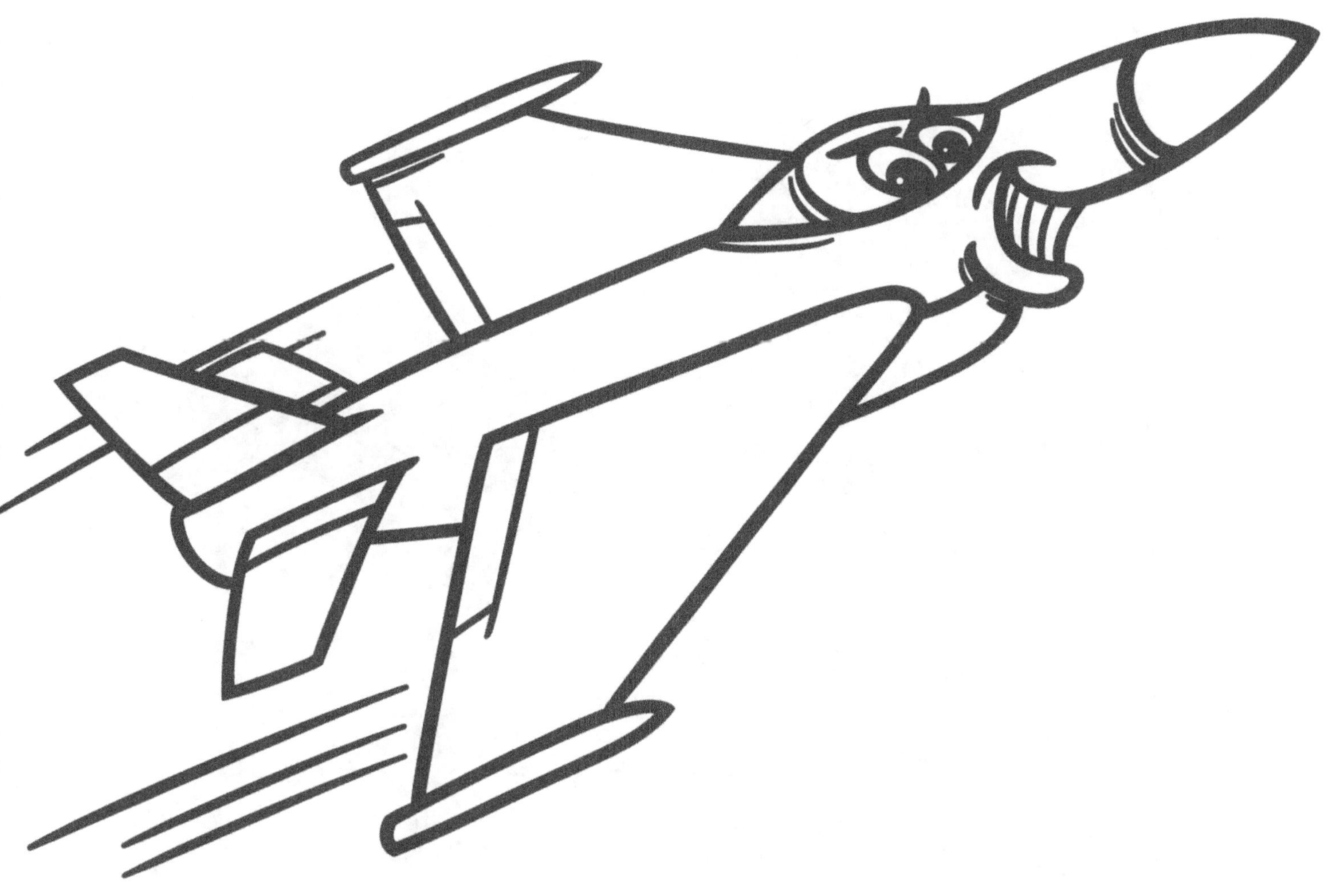

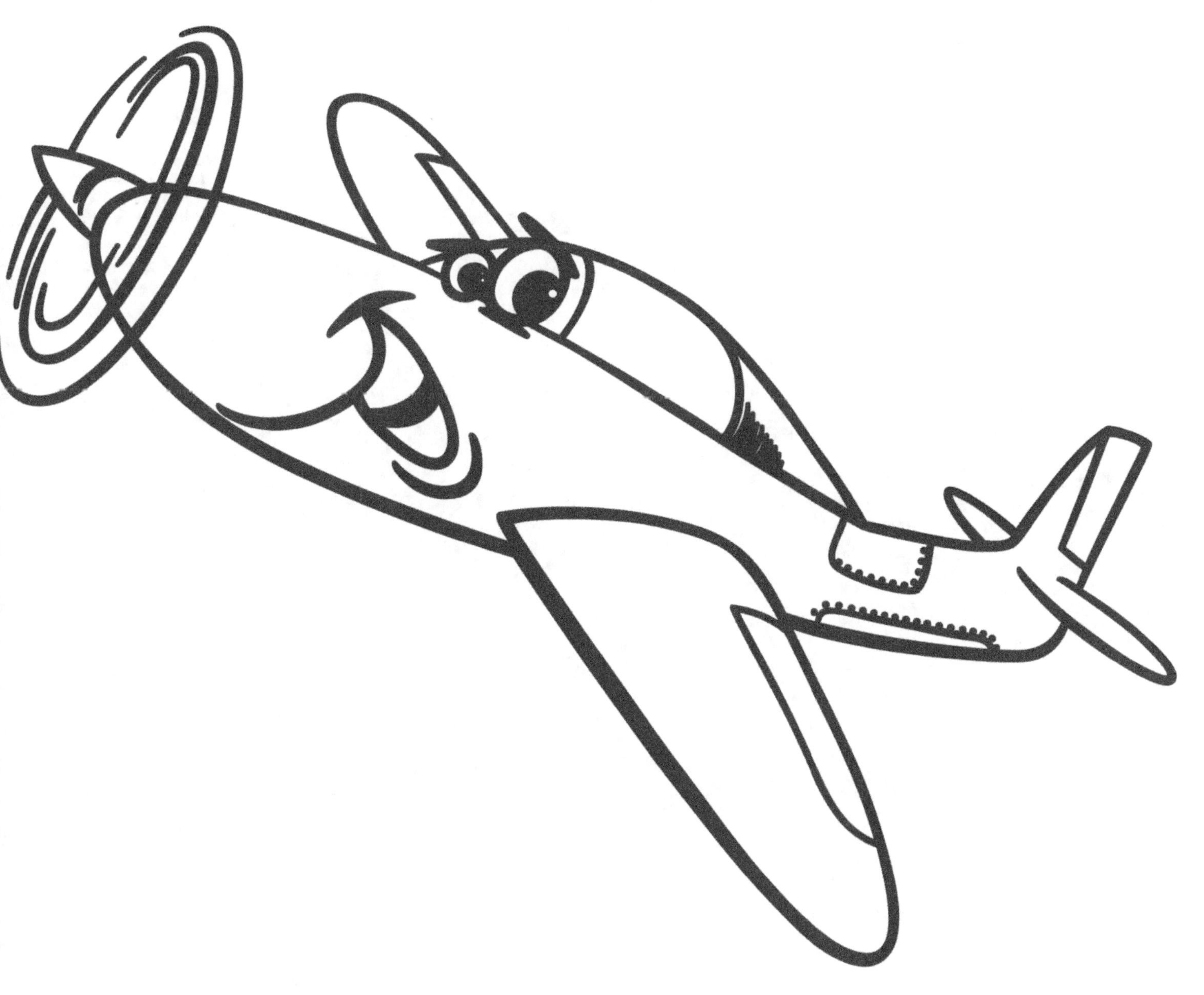

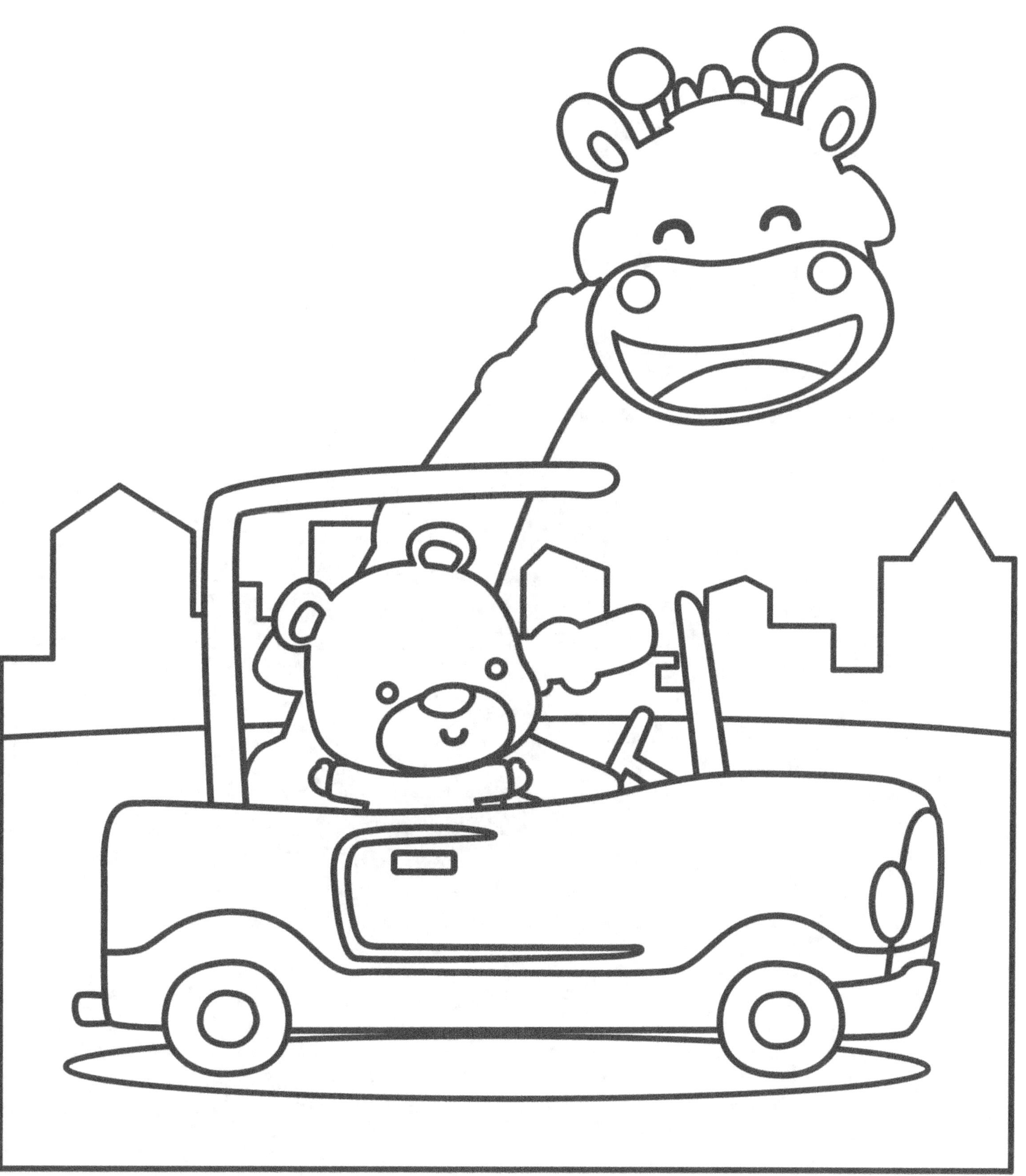

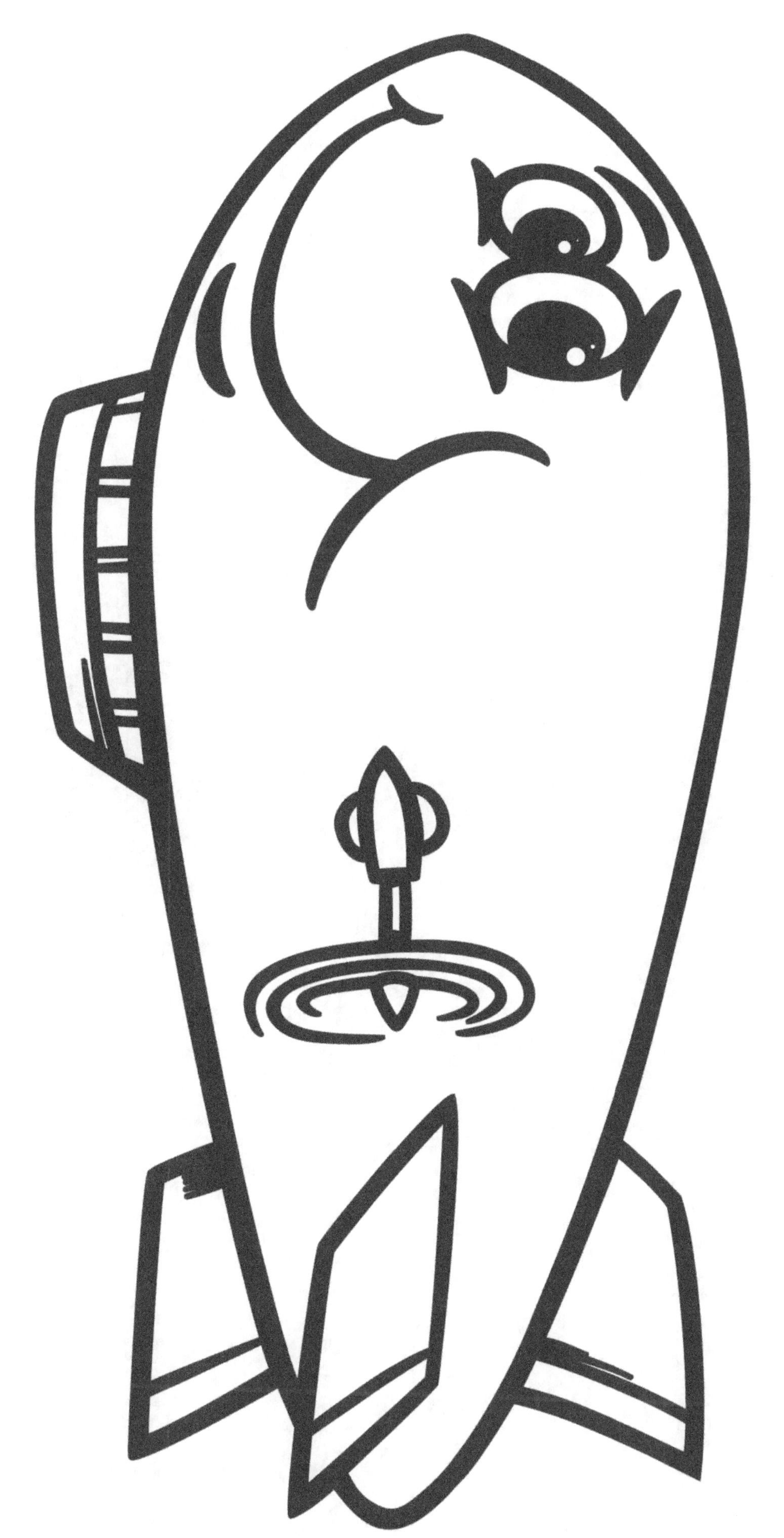

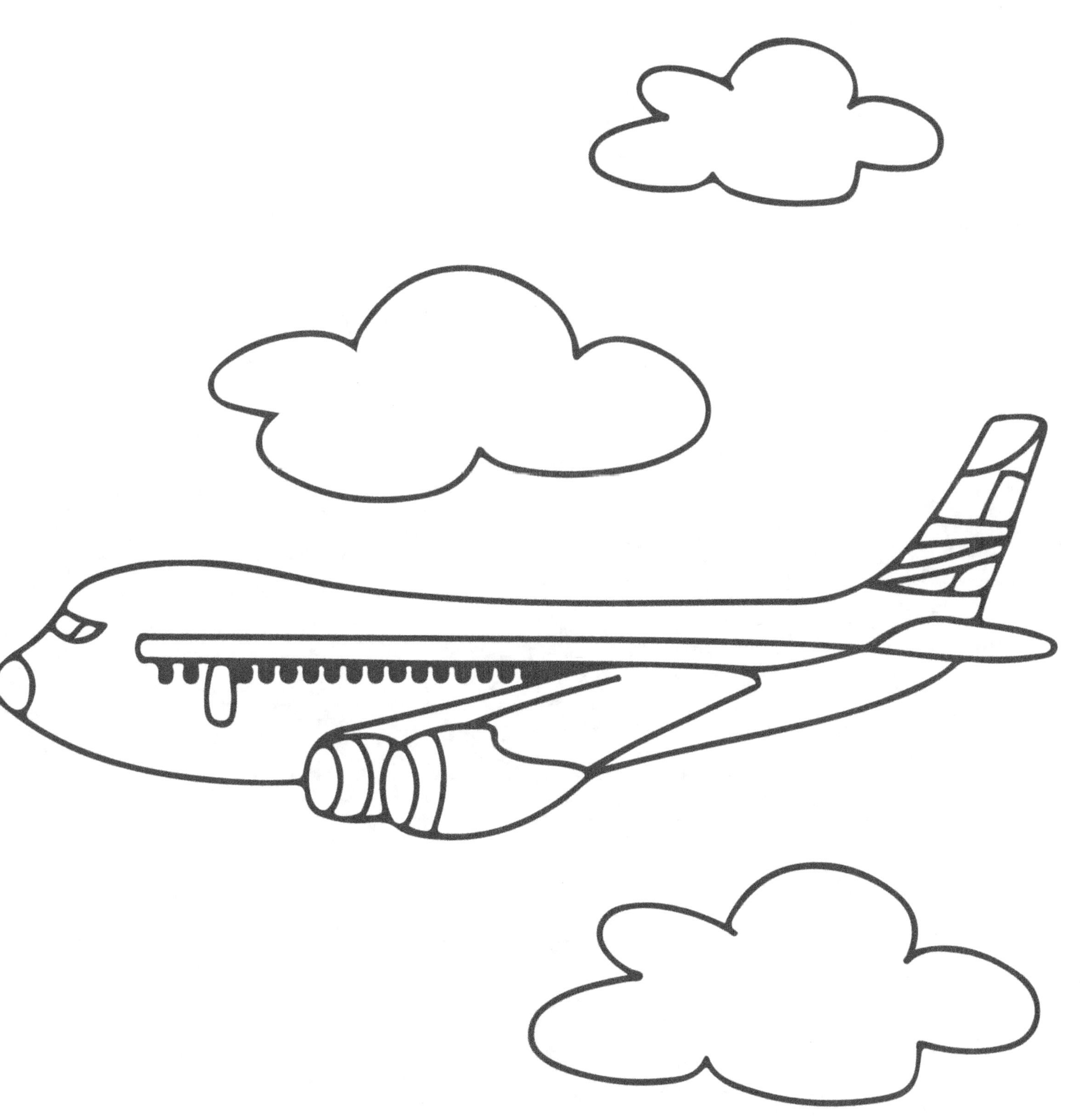